Dreams Unfulfilled:
Stories of the Men and Women on the Vietnam Veterans Memorial

Compiled by Jan C. Scruggs
Founder and President
Vietnam Veterans Memorial Fund

For more information, contact us at our new address:

Vietnam Veterans Memorial Fund
2600 Virginia Ave., NW, Suite 104
Washington, DC 20037
(202) 393-0090
Fax: (202) 393-0029
www.vvmf.org
vvmf@vvmf.org

Cover photo by Daniel Arant
Back cover photo by Dave Scavone

TABLE OF CONTENTS

Foreword
Jan C. Scruggs

The Vietnam Veterans Memorial is names—more than 58,000 names of men and women who were killed or missing in action during the Vietnam War.

Although it was controversial when it was built, the Memorial is now widely considered a successful work of art. To the visitor, it is a stunning reminder of just how many lives were lost during one of our nation's longest and most divisive wars. When you visit the Memorial, the sheer volume of names is inescapable.

Millions of people visit The Wall each year. For some, it is another stop on an agenda filled with tourist attractions. But for others, it is a special visit to see and touch the name of a loved one enshrined forever on our National Mall, maybe to leave a note or personal item in remembrance. Veterans overwhelmed by emotion come to pay their respects. Friends and family remember loved ones lost decades ago. Parents show names to their children and talk about why that person was special.

The Vietnam Veterans Memorial is not just a wall of names to me. When I look at those names, I am reminded that hundreds of them served in the 199th Light Infantry Brigade in Vietnam, as I did. About 25 of the names inscribed in black granite are people I knew well—having either served with them or having known them in my youth. When I go to The Wall, I remember and mourn them. I see their faces. I think of all the dreams they had that were left unfulfilled.

It is important for us to honor these people who served and sacrificed for their country. But, we should also remember that they were people, just like us. They enjoyed crazy adventures with high school friends. They had crushes, fell in love and got married. Some even had children.

They were people with special talents and many goals. Some wanted to be soldiers or pilots; others wanted to be doctors, nurses or ministers. Some excelled at sports. Others liked fast cars or motorcycles. Some had children they cherished and missed when they were away. Others had children they never met.

There are so many stories on The Wall—stories of people as diverse as our nation itself.

That is why the Vietnam Veterans Memorial Fund created this book. We wanted to remind everyone that the names on The Wall are more than names; they represent unique people with hopes, dreams and desires—people who were loved and who are missed every day by someone they left behind.

VVMF is working now to build an Education Center at The Wall on the National Mall, near the Lincoln and Vietnam Veterans Memorials, which will take this concept of remembrance to a new level.

The underground structure will showcase their pictures and tell some of their stories. It will display some of the more than 100,000 items that have been left in tribute at The Wall since it was dedicated.

The Education Center will honor those who served and sacrificed not just in Vietnam, but in all of America's wars—including those who are in harm's way today, in Iraq and Afghanistan.

We are hoping that the American public will support

this project and help us collect photos and stories. Visit *www.buildthecenter.org* to learn more.

In this book, our contributors wrote about their family members, their friends and the people they served with. There is a special section with stories written by those who never met the people whose names are on The Wall, but were inspired by them.

Another section contains stories about people who died later as a result of the Vietnam War—from conditions such as cancer caused by Agent Orange exposure and complications from post traumatic stress disorder. Although their names are not on The Wall, their sacrifices are no less great.

The men and women who served and sacrificed in Vietnam, whether they came home or not, were an extraordinary group of people. I hope you enjoy reading about some of them.

They Served With Us

An American Hero
By
Gen. Barry R. McCaffrey, USA (Ret.)

1st Lt. David Ragin was my brother-in-law and my hero. He was killed in action (KIA) on Aug. 24, 1964 in a bloody battle along with three other brave American advisors serving with the Vietnamese 41st Ranger Battalion in Kien Hoa Province, 45 miles southwest of Saigon. The Rangers suffered more than 200 casualties during this violent ambush.

All four received the Distinguished Service Cross, the nation's second-highest award for valor. In addition to Dave, the advisors included Capt. Byron Clark Stone, Capt. James Michael Coyle and Sgt. 1st Class Tom Ward.

Dave received the Distinguished Service Cross for his actions during this terrible one-hour and 40-minute battle, in which the Viet Cong conducted four major assaults on the Ranger positions. With aggressive courage during the firefight, he killed more than 30 enemy soldiers. He was last seen alive firing a machine gun while covering the withdrawal of his unit. Dave was 25 when he died in the service of his country. He was promoted to captain after his death.

No one was surprised at Dave's courageous death. He was a senior-ranking cadet at The Citadel, class of 1961. He graduated from Palatka (Florida) High School in 1957 as a very popular and respected student who was a superb athlete and the captain of the football team. The National Guard Armory was named in his honor after his death.

Dave married my sister in 1961 following his graduation from The Citadel. He completed Ranger School and Airborne School at Ft. Benning, Ga. Dave then served with great distinction as an infantry officer in the 101st Airborne Division at Ft. Campbell, Ky. He was given early command of a company and named best company commander in the division prior to volunteering for Vietnam duty.

Dave and my sister had two daughters. Beth has become an accomplished businesswoman. Daughter Lisa Ann, whom he never saw, died 55 days after Dave was killed and was buried in his arms at Arlington National Cemetery.

The officer who escorted Dave's body home from combat was his dear friend and high school classmate, Capt. Henry A. Deutsch. Henry returned to combat in Vietnam and was subsequently killed in action on May 11, 1965.

When Dave was killed, there had only been 189 other Americans KIA in the Republic of Vietnam. The loss of the entire advisory team to 41st Ranger Battalion was a great shock to the country and widely covered in the press at the time. By 1968, we were suffering more than 1,200 killed in action each month. By the end of the war, more than 58,000 brave service men and women had perished in Vietnam, and 304,000 were wounded during this longest American war.

Shortly before Dave deployed, he and I spent half the night talking. I was a cadet at West Point and had enormous respect for this dedicated and confident young officer. Dave was filled with enthusiasm and spirit. His dad had fought in World War II, and he wanted to join the long line of American patriots who had served to keep us free. His promising life was cut so short. All of us who knew and served with him are better because of his example of integrity, service and courage.

The caption under David Ragin's picture in his high school yearbook is his enduring epitaph: "He is so good that no one can be a better man."

WILLIAM DAVID HOWSA RAGIN is honored on Panel 1E, Row 62 of the Vietnam Veterans Memorial.

GEN. BARRY McCAFFREY, USA (Ret.) served 32 years of active military duty with four combat tours, including advisory duty with the Army of the Republic of Vietnam from 1966–67 and company command with the 1st Cavalry Division in Vietnam from 1968-69. He was twice awarded the Distinguished Service Cross, received two Silver Star medals and was awarded three Purple Heart medals for wounds received in infantry combat.

Gen. McCaffrey is a member of VVMF's Corporate Council and is the chairman of the Advisory Board for the Education Center at The Wall. In January 2010, he chaired a delegation of veterans and their families who returned to Vietnam to observe the operations of VVMF's international humanitarian program there, Project RENEW.

Two Outstanding and Heroic Marine Corporals
By
Marshall N. Carter

When you serve your country and go into combat, regardless of service branch, you work with, lead and follow outstanding young men and women. This was true in Vietnam, just as it was in all prior American wars—and as it is today. Our young service members are just outstanding and always have been. It can be difficult to single out any one individual, but on occasion, there are those who deserve to be held out as lifelong examples for the rest of us.

In my case, having served for two years in Vietnam as a Marine Corps junior infantry officer, I had numerous occasions to observe many other Marines. Two stand out above all the rest: Cpl. Jack Sutton and Cpl. Jim Cannington.

Jack Sutton was 21 and an outstanding leader in combat. He was well known in the Harvey, Ill., area for his athletic prowess. At Thornton Township High School, Jack earned 12 letters in sports, was named Most Outstanding Player in football and was well-known for his wrestling ability, because he was 6 feet tall and weighed 285 pounds.

He trimmed down to join the Marines in February 1966, arriving in Vietnam in late August of that year. He was wounded twice while leading his squad of 14 Marines.

A young man with great leadership abilities, he routinely exposed himself to enemy fire to ensure the safety of his men and the accomplishment of their mission.

Jim Cannington, age 19, was born in Lennox, Ga., and grew up in Baltimore, Md. He loved the water and, at 17, was a certified rescue diver for the local fire department water rescue. Jim graduated from Patapsco Senior High School in 1965. He was an active member of the Baptist Church and intended on pursuing a Baptist ministry. He enlisted in the Marine Corps out of high school to follow in his father's footsteps.

Jim arrived in Vietnam on Sept. 23, 1966 and volunteered for extremely dangerous duty, living with and training Vietnamese indigenous troops in the villages as part of the Combined Action Platoon (CAP) program. In the CAP program, U.S. Marines and Navy corpsmen lived and worked with the Vietnamese to teach them better combat effectiveness and learn from them about the local area, people, customs and Viet Cong activity. It was a select program and extremely hazardous.

When he came back to a rifle company, he continued to be an outstanding leader. We all learned quickly that to assign a job or combat mission to Jim was to ensure its completion.

Jack Sutton and Jim Cannington both came from large families and knew the value of teamwork, whether it be with their siblings or with others in combat. These traits were essential to their mission on Jan. 14, 1967.

The company was assigned to conduct a helicopter-borne raid into an enemy stronghold. Immediately upon debarking, they and their squads encountered fierce enemy fire. Both took charge, deployed their men and overcame enemy opposition, greatly aiding the company in taking the objective. On one occasion, Jim Cannington led his men down a dangerous jungle path into the enemy's fortified position, while Jack Sutton singlehandedly held off a large enemy force with a machine gun while his men deployed around the enemy.

Both men performed in a manner that this country has expected of its combat leaders since the Revolutionary War. But unfortunately, on that day in that jungle village, they were both killed while leading. I was proud to serve with them and have remembered them every day since that fateful day in January 1967.

JACK RICHARD SUTTON is honored on Panel 14E, Row 30 of the Vietnam Veterans Memorial.

JAMES B. CANNINGTON JR. is honored on Panel 14E, Row 26 of the Vietnam Veterans Memorial.

MARSHALL N. CARTER served as a Marine Corps rifle company commander in Vietnam from 1966-67. He is the chairman of the New York Stock Exchange. A member of VVMF's Corporate Council, he also supports the group's international humanitarian program in Vietnam, called Project RENEW, and its various initiatives.

Remembering Sgt. Tom Young, USMC
By
Dale Dye

We were sitting in one of the huge old blimp hangars at the Marine Corps Air Facility, Santa Ana, Calif., in the late summer of 1967, contemplating orders to pack our trash and say our goodbyes. We were headed for Vietnam.

Cpl. Tom Young said he thought he'd better submit his leave papers in a hurry and try to squeeze out 30 days with his family back in Arkansas. The anxiety over leave was perfectly understandable. We all knew in those days when the war seemed to be simmering toward a boil, that pre-deployment leave might well be the last any of us saw of our loved ones. But, Tom was even more anxious to get to Vietnam and talked about leave as though it were just an expected step along the way to some momentous journey of discovery.

"Hemingway was right," he once told me. "War is man's greatest adventure." He was the kind of guy who could say things like that without eliciting catcalls and harassment from his fellow Marines.

On a previous tour, I'd seen that elephant and heard that owl, as the saying goes, so I wasn't as romantically inclined about my orders. But Tom was an irrepressible spirit who saw humor and excitement every time the sun rose to bring us another day. I said I would cover our duties at the base and let him get on with it.

As Marine Corps Combat Correspondents, we could be assigned anywhere in-country where Marines operated, as well as in a few interesting billets that did not involve accompanying line units into combat. I got orders to one of the line units, and Tom got assigned to an American Forces Vietnam Network (AFVN) radio and TV outlet in Hue.

I managed to visit him at that station, and he took me on a tour of the city to include a very interesting look at the ancient Citadel on the north side of the Perfume River.

Tom seemed envious of my assignment involving regular combat operations vs. his, which pretty much kept him out of the action. I volunteered to trade places, but Tom—by now a newly-minted sergeant of Marines—felt the experience would help him achieve his goal of studying broadcast journalism at the University of Missouri. It didn't keep me from harassing him about a cushy rear-echelon job and reminding him of his reference to Hemingway's infamous quote.

That meeting was in January 1968. There was no way for either of us to know what lay in store during the Tet Lunar New Year just a few weeks in the future.

When the North Vietnamese Army (NVA) staged its offensive during the country-wide Tet celebrations, Hue was one of their primary targets. Tom and the other civilians, soldiers, sailors, airmen and Marines assigned to the AFVN station were quickly under siege in the first days of the attack on the city. They fought a gallant but hopeless battle with no real reaction plan and minimal firepower as the NVA pressed their attack.

After a gallant stand-off involving vicious firefights, the station was overrun. Six men were captured. Five of them became long-term POWs in North Vietnam. One was captured and then executed. Two were killed in the action—and one of those was my friend Sgt. Tom Young.

Later in the fighting to retake Hue, I was assigned to assault units and managed to get a close look at the battered and shattered AFVN station where I'd visited Tom prior to Tet. The evidence was clear: the NVA made a major effort to take the station, and the people resisting that effort had put up a hell of a fight to prevent it. It was cold comfort for the loss of a friend, but it was obvious that Sgt. Tom Young had experienced man's greatest adventure—and greatest tragedy.

THOMAS FRANKLIN YOUNG is honored on Panel 37E, Row 16 of the Vietnam Veterans Memorial.

DALE DYE joined the U.S. Marine Corps in 1964 and served as a Marine Correspondent in Vietnam during 1967-70, surviving 31 major combat operations. During the war, he received a Bronze Star and three Purple Hearts for wounds suffered in combat. He spent 13 years as an enlisted Marine, until he was chosen for Officer Candidate School and was appointed a warrant officer in 1976. He retired in 1984 at the rank of captain.

Dye founded Warriors, Inc., a California firm that specializes in training actors for realistic military portrayals in war movies. He has also acted in some of these movies, including "Platoon," "Saving Private Ryan," "Band of Brothers" and "The Pacific."

The Only U.S. Military Woman KIA in Vietnam
By
Janie Blankenship

Although seven other American female military nurses died while serving in Vietnam, Sharon Ann Lane was the only U.S. servicewoman killed as a direct result of enemy fire during the war.

On June 8, 1969, the 312th Evacuation Hospital was struck by a salvo of 122 mm rockets fired by the Viet Cong. One rocket struck between Wards 4A and 4B, killing two other Americans and wounding 27. Lane died instantly of fragmentation wounds to the chest. At 25 years old, she was buried with full military honors in Canton, Ohio.

Lane was born on July 7, 1943 in Zanesville, Ohio. Her family moved to Canton, where she attended high school.

She graduated from Aultman Hospital School of Nursing in Canton in 1965. Following two years of clinical practice as a general duty nurse, Lane entered the Army Nurse Corps in 1968.

After completing basic training at Brooke Army Medical Center in Fort Sam Houston, Texas as a second lieutenant, she was assigned to the U.S. Army Fitzsimmons General Hospital in Denver, Colo. After receiving a promotion to first lieutenant, she was placed in the cardiac division's intensive care unit (ICU) and recovery room. Lane also volunteered to nurse the most critically injured American soldiers in the surgical ICU in her off-duty hours. She worked in the ICU until sent to Vietnam.

On April 26, 1969, Lane arrived at the 312th Evacuation Hospital in Chu Lai. Although nursing in Ward 4 was challenging, Lane repeatedly declined transfer to another ward. She also volunteered to care for the most critically wounded GIs in the surgical ICU.

Posthumously, Lane was awarded a Purple Heart, Bronze Star with "V" device and the South Vietnamese Cross of Gallantry with Palm.

In 1969, the Daughters of the American Revolution named Lane "Outstanding Nurse of the Year." In 1970, the Recovery Room at Fitzsimmons Army Hospital was dedicated in her honor, and the Aultman Hospital erected a bronze statue of Lane in 1973. The names of 110 local servicemen killed in Vietnam are on the base of the statue.

In 1986, Aultman Hospital opened the Sharon Ann Lane Womens Center. Fort Hood, Texas, dedicated the Sharon Ann Lane Volunteer Center in 1995. The Sharon Ann Lane Foundation completed and dedicated the Sharon Ann Lane Foundation Clinic in Chu Lai in 2002.

SHARON ANN LANE is honored on Panel 23W, Row 112 of the Vietnam Veterans Memorial.

JANIE BLANKENSHIP is the associate editor for VFW *magazine. This article is reprinted with permission from* VFW *magazine's 2008 special publication,* Women At War.

Remembering Max
By
Justin "Jerry" Martin

Over the last 42 years, I have been asked many times, "How can you be so close to guys you served with for only a year of your life?" For all combat veterans, I imagine the response is similar: "Unless you were there, you wouldn't understand."

For United States Marines, the term "brotherhood" means more than just the men you served with—it has a meaning that is defined by a legacy of over 230 years of service to our nation.

"Brotherhood" evolved into a code of conduct and commitment to each other, mostly unwritten and unspoken, but ingrained in every recruit and officer candidate from their first day of training. It is sealed in the hardships endured by every generation of Marines that has come before and is expected of every generation that comes after. It is the basis for the silent bond that exists between all Marines.

I was inducted into that Brotherhood in the fall of 1967 and would meet the "brothers" with whom I would share the most memorable year of my life in May 1968. I was introduced as the new lieutenant and second platoon commander, and this was sufficient for acceptance into my new family. Two of us were joining the platoon as replacements that day: me and Pfc. Muriel Stanley Groomes—"Max," as he preferred to be called.

Our platoon and their rifle company had only days

before been battered by a numerically superior North Vietnamese infantry regiment for 48 hours of vicious assaults reminiscent of World War II and Korean War battles. A total of 57 Marines were killed or wounded in what became known as the battle for Foxtrot Ridge in the Khe Sanh area of I Corps Republic of Vietnam. It was into this Brotherhood of survivors that Max Groomes and I were thrust for our tour in-country.

Besides being new guys in the platoon, Max and I both came from the same area of the country: Max from Hampstead, Md., and me from Manassas, Va.

There was only three years difference in our ages—he was 19 and I was 22—yet he referred to me respectfully as "Lieutenant" or "The Old Man" (with a smile) when I later became the company commander. I referred to him as "Little Brother" because our interpreter had told me that the Vietnamese word for an enlisted man was "*anh em*," which means "little brother." It was appropriate; I was the big brother responsible for taking care of and watching out for him and my other men.

However, Max was not the typical Marine. He was small in frame and, others later said, too kind and gentle in nature to be in combat.

My recollections of Max are of a Marine who was always willing to do more than what was expected of him. On patrol, even when suffering from both malaria and active dysentery, he willingly shouldered another Marine's heavy machine gun when that Marine complained of not being able to make it. Max willingly shared the contents of his packages from home and gave away his rations of beer and cigarettes. He often volunteered to carry the platoon radio when others balked at the task, even though he realized this made him more of an enemy target than his job as a rifleman did. He was selfless in nature, always willing to do his job without complaint and usually with a shy smile. Seldom did he speak of home except an occasional mention of older brothers, a fondness for Maryland seafood and a desire to get back to "the world," our slang term for the United States.

He was the quietest member of our small portion of the Brotherhood. There was no pretense or false bravado about him. Max listened more than he talked. His actions were more memorable than his conversations. He was just a damn good Marine.

As a combat leader, I learned to steel my emotions to the news of casualties in our unit. However, shortly after I left the rifle company and was awaiting reassignment, I was notified that one of my men had been killed in action. I ran to the landing zone to check on the casualties evacuated to the battalion aid station, and there was Max, his shattered remains wrapped in a poncho and guarded by the sergeant who had been wounded with him.

Both men had absorbed the blast of a command-detonated claymore mine. One Marine had lived; the other had died. Max had volunteered to carry the radio that day. Typical of Max, he had helped someone else and then made the ultimate sacrifice.

Muriel Stanley Groomes is an unsung American patriot. His name is but one of the many listed on what Vietnam veterans call our "hallowed ground"—the Vietnam Veterans Memorial. His service and sacrifice are anonymous, except for the posthumous Purple Heart awarded in his memory to his next of kin. His courage and life are remembered only by those who knew him. His death was not heroic, but was selfless, like Max himself.

Max Groomes represents just one of the thousands who stand in silent witness to the devotion to duty displayed by a generation of Americans. When those who knew him are gone, who will speak for him? I hope that, in my lifetime, a Vietnam Veterans Memorial Education Center will be built to honor those like Lance Cpl. Muriel Stanley Groomes. Semper Fidelis, Max.

MURIEL STANLEY GROOMES is honored on Panel 39W, Row 8 of the Vietnam Veterans Memorial.

JUSTIN "JERRY" MARTIN is a retired Marine Corps lieutenant colonel and Vietnam veteran. Among his combat decorations are the Silver Star for gallantry and the Purple Heart. He is also a retired Virginia public high school teacher and was a member of the inaugural class of VVMF's Teach Vietnam Teachers Network. He has brought numerous students to participate in VVMF activities over the years.

I Don't Remember His Name
By
Sara McVicker

The medical patients usually came in late afternoon. They'd send a chopper around to the firebases if anyone needed to come in to the hospital. Most would be an FUO (fever of unknown origin, which usually would turn out to be malaria or typhus), sometimes dysentery, occasionally pneumonia, and once or twice a cardiac case.

Unless they were so woozy they couldn't stand up, we would get the blood samples we needed for diagnosis, let them shower, feed them and then let them sleep as much as possible around monitoring their temperatures and getting additional malaria smears. Most of them weren't too sick—sick enough to be sent to the hospital, but not critical.

After diagnosis and treatment, they sometimes went straight back to the field, or if they were lucky, they got a week or so at the 6th Convalescent Center in Cam Rahn Bay. That's probably why I don't remember names. I didn't want to pick up a *Stars and Stripes* and see that someone we had sent back to the field had gotten killed.

One afternoon, a call came from the ER: FUO, unconscious, temperature off the end of the thermometer. They did not have much history on the patient. He was out in the boonies with his unit and hadn't felt good for a couple of days, but nothing specific. Then suddenly he collapsed, burning up to the touch. They threw him in a mud puddle to try to get his temperature down and called in a "dust off" (the helicopter that would take him to the hospital).

They brought him up from the ER on a stretcher, packed in bags of ice. We got all the diagnostic tests, got another IV in him and a urinary catheter. Jim, our chief of medicine, was the doc.

We started him on quinine in case he had malaria. We gave him something for typhus and something else for a bacterial infection. None of the tests showed anything in particular. We kept sponging him down and, between that and the aspirin suppositories, his temperature started coming down.

A little before 7 p.m., the night nurse and corpsman came in and saw what was going on. I asked the nurse to handle the rest of the ward. I hadn't done any 6:00 meds, but one of the corpsmen had done vital signs, kept an eye on the IVs, gotten everyone fed and had told me everyone else was OK. All the other patients knew what was going on.

Finally, we had done everything we could. His temperature had come down, and we had gotten him cleaned up. I gave a report to the night nurse and then went back in the room to see if Jim needed me for anything else before I left. No, he said, but he thought that he would stay for a while.

The next morning when I came back, Jim was still there. He had stayed by this guy's side all night, and he was there almost all that day, too, except for a few breaks. The patient was still unconscious but stable.

And then he began to slip away from us. It was nothing dramatic, just blood pressure gradually dropping, urine output decreasing. No heroics—there wasn't anything else to be done. And then, he was gone.

We never knew what killed him, whether it was whatever caused his fever or if it was because the fever was so high it "zapped" his brain.

I don't remember his name or where he was from, but I know where he is now. His name is somewhere on the west Wall of the Vietnam Veterans Memorial, panels 26-19.

He didn't die alone.

And I remember him.

SARA McVICKER served in the Army Nurse Corps from 1968-71, including a tour in Vietnam from 1969-70 at the 71st Evacuation Hospital in Pleiku. Afterward, she worked for the Department of Veterans Affairs for 27 years before retiring in 2006. She is a volunteer for VVMF and serves on the Advisory Board for the Education Center at The Wall.

They Were Our Family

A Simple Day
By
Yolanda Acevedo

Dad and I left the house early. As always, we had breakfast together. It was still dark outside, but I did not care. That day was going to be just Dad and me.

As we went through the base gates, there was a soldier there. At that moment, I realized that they were always there, a familiar and constant feature in my childhood universe. We went to Dad's office and said hello to different people. Most I recognized; some I did not. Many had been to our house on different occasions—for parties, to say hello or just to talk. It was 1968, and we were in the middle of the Vietnam War. I guess that during difficult times and being far away from home, friends became family. I remember back then, we had a lot of family!

It was a beautiful spring day in paradise. After lunch, Dad and I played golf. I had never played golf before that day. I think that, like many things in life, golf is something that you either like or you don't. I do not like golf. I never have.

That day, however, it was different. That day, I loved golf. It was our special day, and for a little girl who adored her father, it was heaven. Dad tried to teach me to play the game he loved, and I loved every minute of it. We talked, walked and laughed all through the golf course while trying unsuccessfully to play. We shared stories and dreams all day long.

It was the perfect day, just my best friend and me.

As time passes by, some memories start to fade, while others remain. I have many memories of Dad, but the images and feelings of that day will stay with me forever.

Years later, I learned that Dad had received deployment orders just a week before our little outing. He was going to Vietnam. He was going to leave me behind. Soon after, he was gone! I was alone and, for the first time, I experienced loneliness. There would be no more breakfasts together, no more playing golf or singing, and no more walks for Dad and me. He left, never to come back.

Among the personal items returned to us by the Army were pieces of Dad's rosary. He always wore it around his neck. Years later, I decided to put together the remaining pieces. On my wedding day, I hid it in my bouquet. No one knew.

We were deprived of so many days, but not that day. In a very simple and quiet way, he walked down the aisle with me.

We had one more walk together, Dad and me.

JOSE L. MONTES is honored on Panel 41W, Row 25 of the Vietnam Veterans Memorial.

YOLANDA ACEVEDO lives in Virginia with her two children. She lost her husband, Navy Commander Joseph Acevedo, in Bahrain in 2003 during Operation Iraqi Freedom. She serves as a peer mentor for the Tragedy Assistance Program for Survivors (TAPS), a national non-profit organization that provides services to those who have lost a loved one on active duty in the armed forces. She is also a member of Sons and Daughters in Touch (SDIT), a group of children of the men whose names are on The Wall, and spoke at the Father's Day Rose Remembrance Ceremony at The Wall in 2006.

My Cousin Jean
By
Lt. Col. Janis Nark, USAR (Ret.)

Jean Mason Kraus was the youngest of three exceptional boys who were my favorite cousins. They were teenagers back then: fun, handsome, intelligent, full of life. I was six years younger and rarely, if ever, noticed by them.

Every summer when I was young, we would pile into the Ford and drive from Detroit to Grandma and Grandpa Mason's farm in Novelty, Mo. That constituted our official summer vacation trip.

When we first started that tradition, water at the farm was drawn from the well, and the toilet was through the chicken yard along a wooden-planked path to the outhouse. We thought this was great adventure. There were cows, pigs, horses and chickens. The food on our dining table came from all but the horses, and the rest came from the fields and my grandmother's garden out back. She used the *Farmer's Almanac* and planted by the moon. She grew the sweetest sweet corn and the biggest, ripest, reddest, most delicious tomatoes in the world.

My favorite relatives lived near Lake of the Ozarks, and it was always a time of great excitement and fun when we could go visit them. Aunt Marie was the mother of the three outstanding young men: my cousins Jean, Bill and Sam. She was short, pudgy, outgoing, warm and funny. She personified love like no one I'd ever known in my short life. They had a homemade pond with a raft in the middle where we'd all go swimming in those peaceful days of the 1950s.

It was a special treat to go to Lake of the Ozarks. We would go boating with our relatives on the lake, as the old 8 mm movies from that time show us doing over and over again. In one of those movies, I'm sitting next to cousin Jean in the back of the boat as it's leaving the dock. I'm trailing my fingers in the water, imagining that I look very much like Marilyn Monroe. What I look like is a very geeky kid with a frizzy home perm. He is oblivious to me, and I am madly in love with him.

Jean went on to college and became a teacher and an incredibly talented artist. He painted beautiful, tranquil and deeply emotional pieces in oils and watercolors. The ones I saw were always scenes of nature, of rivers, of the land he so loved.

When he was drafted, it never occurred to him not to go. He didn't choose to be an officer, though that was offered. No, he would just go, do his duty and then come home to his life of teaching and painting. He wasn't meant to be a soldier; he was a soft, kind and gentle spirit. The Army made him a grunt.

I had joined the Army in nursing school and was at my first duty station, Madigan General Hospital at Ft. Lewis, Wash., in 1970. We were busy of course, with busloads of wounded Vietnam vets coming into our wards daily. I was young and naïve, but getting older every day.

My parents came to visit from Michigan, and I enjoyed remembering and feeling what life was like before the Army and the war. Then they told me that cousin Jean had died in Vietnam the week before. All the report said was that he died instantly when he stepped on a booby trap.

My heart broke into a million pieces. One more beautiful soul was gone.

I know his paintings live on. I know that those children whose lives he touched, even briefly, are better for knowing him.

I miss him still.

JEAN MASON KRAUS is honored on Panel 8W, Row 86 of the Vietnam Veterans Memorial.

LT. COL. JANIS NARK, USAR (Ret.) served as a registered nurse in the U.S. Army, including a tour in Vietnam. Later in the Army Reserves, she was recalled to active duty for nine months during Desert Storm. She retired after 26 years. She is a member VVMF's board of directors and is the vice chair of the Education Center at The Wall Advisory Board.

He Was Brilliant—and Nice
By
Col. Alexander P. Shine, USA (Ret.) and
Gail Caprio

On Oct. 15, 1970, Army 1st Lt. Jonathan C. Shine was leading his platoon of the 25th Infantry Division in the Iron Triangle area of Vietnam when they became engaged in a fierce firefight with a much larger enemy force. Ignoring a head wound, Jon encouraged the platoon medic to take care of another soldier. A few minutes later, Lt. Shine was dead.

Those who knew Jon during his school days would remember him as a multi-talented young man. Consistently a top student, he was a "Star Man"—in the top 5 percent of his class—all four years at West Point. Jon was also an athlete and leader. But the qualities which most stood out in Jon were his integrity and his warm friendliness and interest in everyone he met.

People respected Jon because he lived in accordance with a high code of integrity and honor; and they liked him because he genuinely liked them, whatever their status or position in life. As a West Point classmate said of him, "Jon Shine was a class act."

As president of his Briarcliff, N.Y., high school student body, Jon and his equally talented vice president, Gail Morrison, stood at the top of their class, while also developing a friendship which grew deeper and led to their marriage in February 1970. Only a few months later, Jon shipped out for Vietnam.

Gail was attending the funeral of one of their friends,

another soldier, when the news of Jon's death reached her. With the courage of a soldier's wife and faith in God, Gail rallied and was an encouragement to many others as the body of this outstanding young man, and the love of her life, was laid to rest in the West Point cemetery.

The youngest of four siblings—all of whom served in Vietnam—Jon was the first to be killed, but sadly he would not be the last. A little over two years later, the oldest of the Shine children, Lt. Col. Anthony Shine, an Air Force fighter pilot, went down during a bombing run and was missing in action for nearly 25 years before his remains were recovered and buried with full honors in Arlington National Cemetery.

Any description of Jon Shine would be incomplete without mention of the central focus of his adult life: his strong and steadfast Christian faith. Jon surrendered his life to Jesus Christ as a plebe at West Point and, consistently through his cadet years and the 16 months of Army service that followed, he sought to live a life that would serve men and bring honor to God. In a letter to his brother Al, who was serving in Vietnam during Jon's senior year at West Point, Jon quoted Psalm 27:1: *"The Lord is my light and my salvation – whom shall I fear? The Lord is the strength of my life – of whom shall I be afraid?"* He faced life and death with courage born of confidence in the Lord.

As his widow, Gail, said of Jon, "He was brilliant; but he was nicer than he was brilliant."

JONATHAN CAMERON SHINE is honored on Panel 6W, Row 2 of the Vietnam Veterans Memorial.

This remembrance was written by his brother, COL. ALEXANDER P. SHINE, USA (Ret.) and his widow, Ms. GAIL CAPRIO. Those interested in knowing more about Jon Shine are encouraged to read a book focused on his life, Out of the Valley, *which can be purchased from the Officer's Christian Fellowship, www.ocfusa.org.*

Overcoming Incredible Odds
By
Anthony, Colleen, Shannon and
Bomette "Bonnie" Shine

Before volunteering for his second tour of duty in Vietnam, before escorting his youngest brother's body home for burial, even before joining the United States Air Force in 1961, Tony Shine was a man of character and perseverance. He was a big man, standing a few inches above 6 feet and weighing in at 230 pounds. Physical fitness was his lifelong tenet for being the best he could be.

In grade school, Tony was handsome and smart, the consummate Norman Rockwell picture of a healthy, vibrant "boy's boy." Fittingly, his first love before flying was football. Tony relished the competition, team discipline and excitement of the game. When he was 11, tragedy struck Tony in the form of polio, a crippling disease that struck fear in the hearts of families across the United States. So many who contracted the disease would be paralyzed by it; some would die from it.

Tony was bedridden with polio for many long months—no more running, blocking or tackling, just lying still, exercising his mind and will to recover. When he finally succeeded in defeating polio, Tony's body was weak and atrophied. His left hand was so badly ravaged that muscle transplant operations were necessary to restore use of his thumb. His physical deterioration was such that he couldn't pick up or hold a pencil with either hand. Doctors explained that the damage to his muscles was so severe he would be lucky to walk normally again, let alone to play football.

Devastated but not defeated, Tony made a decision not to quit. Drawing on a determination and self-discipline that would become his hallmark, he was diligent with his physical therapy, pushing himself to do more and to be more than his doctors deemed possible. In a matter of months, the boy who could not pick up a pencil or write his name, even with his good hand, had overcome the odds. Through tenacity and arduous physical therapy, not only did Tony learn how to write again with his right hand, but he could write equally well with his left.

Once he could stand, Tony rebuilt his body and his life. He learned to walk without a limp and began training so he could try out for his high school football team. At first, it was difficult; the cheerleaders on the sidelines could run up and down the field faster than he could. Yet he never gave up. Eventually, he earned a place as a starting player on the varsity team. And later, he went on to become a starting player in college football for Colgate University.

Following the muscle transplant surgery, growth in Tony's left hand was stunted, and it always remained considerably smaller than his right. This malady could have disqualified him from being an Air Force pilot, let alone a fighter pilot, with its uniquely stringent physical requirements. Again, Tony met the challenge and overcame it. He used weights and, for years, carried hand grips in his coat pockets so he could exercise his left hand.

Early in his Air Force career, Tony served as an instructor pilot. Leading by word and example, he encouraged his students to work harder and to persevere to reach their goals. Drawing on his personal experiences and one of his favorite poems by Rudyard Kipling, "If," Tony challenged his students. Sometimes, he would say, you must "force your heart and nerve and sinew to serve your turn long after they are gone, and so hold on when there is nothing in you except the will which says to them 'hold on.'"

Lt. Col. Anthony C. Shine, USAF, was missing in action from 1972-1996, when his remains were repatriated and interred at Arlington National Cemetery. The U.S. Air Force's top gun award, the *Lt. Col. Anthony C. Shine Award*, is presented annually to the USAF fighter pilot who most exemplifies Tony's caliber of character and his professionalism in flying a tactical fighter aircraft.

ANTHONY CAMERON SHINE is honored on Panel 1W, Row 93 of the Vietnam Veterans Memorial.

This article was written by Anthony Shine's children— ANTHONY W. SHINE, COLLEEN C. SHINE and SHANNON SHINE—and their mother, BOMETTE "BONNIE" SHINE. The Shine family remains dedicated to the fullest possible accounting for America's prisoners and missing. Visit: www.pow-miafamilies. org.

Living Life to the Fullest
By
Judy C. Campbell

Live, laugh, love. When I think of my brother Keith Allen Campbell, I think of those three words. Keith was the epitome of someone who lived life to its fullest.

Sadly, he left this earth on Feb. 8, 1967, while serving in the U.S. Army in Vietnam with the 173d Airborne Brigade (Sep.). An Army medic, he used his body as a shield to protect a fellow soldier after he had provided life-saving medical treatment.

Keith had already served in the Dominican Republic with the 82nd Airborne Division and had received his honorable discharge. But he re-enlisted as the Vietnam conflict heated up, because, he said, "My medic skills are needed."

Long before he was an Army medic, he was my big brother. I vividly remember playing with my Barbie and Ginny dolls, taking a blanket and cardboard to partition off rooms as if I were making my own little dollhouse. Often, I was teased for this—playing with dolls long after many of my girlfriends became interested in boys—but Keith never teased me. Instead, he often made splints for my dolls, as I pretended they fell and broke a leg or arm.

Keith always wanted to become an Army doctor, and I wanted to become a nurse; we shared a common bond in this field. His Boy Scout Troop #165 at Mt. Olivet Church in Arlington, Va., always won the first aid competitions because of Keith's efforts. In addition to giving medical treatment to my dolls, he also helped patch up the local kids as he got older. I was always his ready and willing nurse, no matter who the patients were!

Our mother, Esther B. Campbell Gates, saw Keith's interest in medicine early on and invested in a set of medical encyclopedias, which Keith read cover to cover several times. Later, when my children were growing up, I would often reference these books.

Over the years, Keith caught me opening my Christmas presents early, then rewrapping them so no one would know I had been peeking. I just could not wait for Christmas morning! He liked trying to frustrate my attempts at getting a preview of my gifts—for instance, taking an entire roll of Scotch tape to wrap my gift.

But, I will never forget Christmas 1961; I think Keith was more excited than I was! Our front hallway door was always open, so it was not unusual for it to be open that Christmas morning. But for some reason, Keith kept an eye on it, making sure nobody closed it. We began taking turns opening our gifts, and when it was my turn, Keith said, "Judy, go close the hallway door."

When I did, there behind the door was a life-sized doll for me! She was the size of a three-year-old child. I still have "Peggy," as we named her, and now my granddaughters play with her.

Keith was not only my big brother, but he was also a

father figure, someone I truly looked up to for advice. I was amazed at how many people loved and respected him. He was adventuresome, but not reckless or careless. School bored Keith, as he was a hands-on type of guy and in many ways was self-educated.

Being a medic in the Army was just the first step in my brother's life plan, in which he eventually saw himself becoming a doctor.

While he never was able to complete all he wanted to do, he did use his medical skills to help many people before he died. While on maneuvers with the 11th Special Forces, his first sergeant walked into a tree limb. Keith immediately knew that time was of the utmost importance and surgically removed the limb, saving his vision. Sgt. Wood remains in contact with our family to this day.

SP4 Keith Allen Campbell gave his all during his life, and his memory will live on for generations to come. In my heart, I will always be honored to say that not only did I know Keith Allen Campbell, but I was blessed to be his baby sister.

KEITH ALLEN CAMPBELL is honored on Panel 15E, Row 8 of the Vietnam Veterans Memorial.

JUDY C. CAMPBELL lives in Wilmington, Del., and is an active participant in VVMF ceremonies and programs, as well as a strong supporter of the Education Center at The Wall. She works tirelessly on behalf of Gold Star Families everywhere.

Keith A. Campbell's memory lives on in many ways. In 2006, the Fort Sam Houston Library was renamed the Keith A. Campbell Memorial Library. Also, the George Washington Chapter of the Association of the U.S. Army issues the Keith A. Campbell Memorial Plaque annually to the outstanding enlisted reservist in the Washington, D.C. area.

An Ideal Son
By
Ann Sherman Wolcott

My son Rex Sherman was born on April 8, 1951, the week of Gen. Douglas MacArthur's famous retirement speech, which included these words: "Old soldiers never die, they just fade away."

Eighteen years later, Rex died as a young soldier in the Republic of Vietnam on Nov. 19, 1969, while serving as an assistant team leader with the 75th Ranger Regiment (Airborne, Long Range Reconnaissance Patrol).

Rex was a happy, healthy boy who had blonde curly hair and sparkling blue eyes. He was a good kid who loved to play soldier and build forts. When he reached school age, he recruited his little brother, who was two and a half years younger, to be his "point man." His job was to warn Rex when Mom was coming so they could stop jumping on the bunk beds — which were draped in blankets and sheets and had become "The Fort."

Rex was always a leader who was loved and respected by his peers and especially by his little brother, Dana. They were inseparable.

On New Years Eve 1962, Rex and Dana were sledding in a park in Pennsylvania. Dana was involved in an accident that pinned his leg between the runners of the sled and a tree. He was seriously injured. Rex instructed a friend to get a blanket and call an ambulance. Then he called me at work to tell me what happened. When

I arrived, Rex had taken care of everything. He was not even 11 years old.

Rex always wanted a car. In 1967, he bought the shell of an old Chevy with no engine for $100, which he had saved from a part-time job. He was 16 and had the dream of putting a hot engine in that car someday. He even bought a new racing steering wheel for it, made out of stainless steel and wood.

He would go out and sit in that old car after school and sometimes at night with his transistor radio—just sit in the car and dream about the day he would get it running. He enlisted in the Army at age 17 and never owned a real vehicle or had a driver's license.

Rex loved music, played guitar and sang. He was in a small band and sang in the school choir.

We were an Army family. His father, Sgt. Lawrence R. Sherman, had a career that took us many places. Rex started his schooling with kindergarten in Germany, then first grade in Alexandria, Va. He went to school in Ohio, West Virginia, Colorado, Kentucky and Pennsylvania. Rex was an average student who opted to serve the country he loved rather than continue his education.

Rex was the ideal son, brother and friend. He was loyal, generous and very patriotic. He had impeccable manners and was very handsome. The girls loved him because of those special traits.

Rex is missed by family and friends every day.

REX MARCEL SHERMAN is honored on Panel 16W, Row 96 of the Vietnam Veterans Memorial. He can be visited at Arlington National Cemetery, Section 36-1313.

ANN SHERMAN WOLCOTT was the national president of the American Gold Star Mothers, Inc. from 2003-04. She is a long-time participant in ceremonies at The Wall and other VVMF activities, and is a vocal advocate of the Education Center at The Wall. She was one of five individuals who filmed public service announcements supporting the Education Center that have aired across the country.

Santa Barbara's Almost-Mayor
By
Tony Cordero

Years before the United States of America was born, Bill Cordero's Spanish explorer ancestors arrived in what is now central California.

The Corderos were one of the original "land grant" families, receiving thousands of acres from the Mexican and Spanish authorities that controlled California prior to its 1850 statehood. By helping construct the iconic California missions, along with their ranching and farming, Mariano, Juan, Adolfo and other early generation Corderos left their fingerprints on Old California.

Bill Cordero was born in Santa Barbara in 1935, a rustic time between the Great Depression and World War II. In their youth, Bill and his sister Dorothy moved to San Pedro, Calif., for a brief time while their father's iron work experience took him to the wartime shipyards of the Port of Los Angeles.

After the war, the family returned to Santa Barbara, and Bill grew to become a Boy Scout, an altar boy and a high school football player. His father's eighth-grade education and work as a blacksmith made Bill yearn for more. He dreamed of being the first of his extended family — seven generations of Californios, many without high school educations — to attend college.

When he was accepted into the Air Force ROTC program at Loyola University in Los Angeles, Bill's life plans were on track. He thought, "I'll graduate from college, obtain my officer's commission and climb the ladder in the U. S. Air Force. After 20 years, I'll retire and return home to become mayor of Santa Barbara." Back then, the seaside community featured an ethnic mix of blue-collar workers and growing middle-class families.

By that calendar, Bill's first run for political office would take place in the late 1970s or early 1980s.

Little did he know that a very different campaign involving his name—and 58,000 others—would be waged in that time frame instead: on Veterans Day 1982, the Vietnam Veterans Memorial would be dedicated to the memories of the more than 58,000 service personnel who gave their lives in the Vietnam War. The war that had divided America for so long would be memorialized on the National Mall, listing the name of every serviceman—and eight service women—in the chronological order that they were taken from us.

But, that was decades in the future. In 1957, Bill married a young Irish girl from Los Angeles, and they quickly began their Hispanic-Irish-Catholic family. They welcomed a daughter and three sons before the 28-year-old Air Force officer left for his first combat tour of Vietnam.

Bill arrived at the Bien Hoa Airbase outside Saigon on the day that President John F. Kennedy was killed in Dallas. As an Air Force navigator, he was among the Air Commandos who served as early advisors to the military forces of the Republic of South Vietnam.

Viewing old photos of the Air Commandos alongside their B-26 bombers gives the impression of a scene from World War II, not the early 1960s in Vietnam. They were living on a jungle air strip, 8,000 miles from home, flying ancient planes that were literally falling apart on them. The conditions then would hardly pass for "modern warfare."

After one tour in Vietnam, Bill's plans were on track. He was credited with combat flying hours, had received commendations for his work, wrote love letters to his wife and inquired about life back in Santa Barbara. "How was the fishing? What's up with the old gang? How was the Old Spanish Days Fiesta?" A growing war in Southeast Asia was on his mind, but his family and Santa Barbara were in his heart.

Santa Barbara, which today is a hideaway for the rich and famous, was originally a town filled with white stucco buildings and red-brick roofs, populated by hard-working people who took pride in their heritage and their community. Bill wanted to balance Santa Barbara's need for progress with respect and honor for its past.

In August 1964, Bill's wife and kids joined him at Clark Air Force Base in the Philippines. Life on the Pacific island was a challenge: weather, food, cinder-block houses, intermittent running water all made for a unique adventure for the family. But they were together, and that was more important than any of the minor inconveniences.

For nearly a year, the family traded road trips throughout the Philippines with two-week intervals when Bill would navigate a two-passenger B-57 to

Saigon for bombing missions over North Vietnam.

As he looked down on the hostile terrain over Vietnam, it appeared vastly different from the views he saw from the cockpit when he was stationed at Oxnard Air Force Base in California and would fly over his boyhood home in the sleepy Santa Barbara hamlet. "The beaches here in Vietnam are the most beautiful I have ever seen," he once wrote.

In June 1965, Bill celebrated an early Father's Day—he and his wife Kay were now expecting their fifth child—and departed for another series of bombing missions in Vietnam.

In the dark, early hours of June 22, 1965, Bill and his pilot Charles Lovelace disappeared in their B-57 while flying over the border of North Vietnam and Laos. Four years later, the wreckage was discovered just inside Laos, in the province of Bolikhamxai.

Despite the mystery of exactly what happened, the nation had lost two warriors; two families had lost their husband and father; and Santa Barbara had lost its future mayor.

Today, Bill Cordero and Charles Lovelace are buried together at Arlington National Cemetery, very close to the Tomb of the Unknowns.

On the Vietnam Veterans Memorial, the names of William E. Cordero and his pilot are inscribed near the top of the second panel, beyond the reach of visitors and tourists, and just high enough to catch the glare of the daytime sun.

WILLIAM EDWARD CORDERO is honored on Panel 2E, Row 15 of the Vietnam Veterans Memorial.

TONY CORDERO lives in San Pedro, Calif. In 1990, he founded Sons and Daughters In Touch, a group dedicated to locating, uniting and providing support for the children of those whose names are on The Wall. He is currently the group's chairman of the board.

His Great Love
By
Jane (Tharp) Woodruff

Earl Watson Tharp Jr. was born on Oct. 3, 1949 to Earl and Billie Tharp. Nineteen months later, on May 17, 1951, Stephen Wayne Tharp was born. I was the last child, born Sept. 20, 1958.

Earl got the baby sister he wanted when I was born. Even though there were nine years between us, we had a bond that defied our age difference. He faithfully loved me and made me feel wanted. I always knew I was special to him. Likewise, he was very special to me. I thought he was great—strong, handsome, generous, patient and kind. I felt safe and secure with him.

Earl was a natural mechanic. In his pre-teen years, without my parents' knowledge, he took apart a Victrola and put it back together. In his teen years, he was an avid motorcycle rider. He was eager to work in high school to save up money for his own car. He could do most of his own repairs on both vehicles.

Earl and I had great fun going on motorcycle rides. He would take me to the Martha Washington Ice Cream Parlor for a treat, just the thing for his 10-year-old sister.

Earl was strong. One of my fond memories is of him challenging me to hit him in the stomach as hard as I could. When I did, I felt like I was hitting a wall. I was so impressed with his strength.

Earl was handsome, and the girls knew it! He would always make sure that his girlfriends treated me well. I think some of them thought I was part of the package and treated me like a little sister.

Earl was generous. While he was in Vietnam, he sent me, his 11-year-old sister who was broke, money to buy Christmas presents. The last letter he sent me, which arrived after his death, included $40 for me to spend however I wished. To me that was a fortune—and a final demonstration of his selflessness.

Earl was patient. I remember when I was five years old, he spent hours with me while I was learning to ride a bicycle, running behind to keep it balanced.

Earl was respectful of authority. He was offended by attitudes and acts of those who participated in anti-war protests. While in Vietnam, he became disillusioned with how our leaders were handling the war, but he maintained a respectful attitude.

My brother was kind. He faithfully wrote letters, always eager to hear news from home. He sent Christmas cards to friends, some of whom were elderly. He and my brother Steve were particularly close. They played together, worked together and were the best of friends. Earl loved hearing all the latest news from Steve, be it college studies, car repairs or finances. When Earl died, Steve not only lost his big brother, but he also lost his best friend.

When Earl graduated from high school, he promptly enlisted in the Army and served with Company B, 229th Aviation Battalion (Assault Helicopter) (Airmobile). He wanted the people of Vietnam to have the freedom we had. He wanted the children of Vietnam to have a better life than their parents.

He was only in Vietnam for a few days before he began counting the days until he would be home.

Given his mechanical skills, it was no surprise to find out that he would be a helicopter gunner and, subsequently, crew chief overseeing maintenance of a helicopter. He took his job very seriously, knowing that a faulty engine could cause the deaths of his comrades.

Earl's fellow soldiers gave him the nickname "Preacher" because of the example he set and his faith in Jesus.

My brother expanded his capacity for love while in Vietnam. On June 26, 1970, he demonstrated this with honor when his base came under heavy rocket and mortar attack.

Earl made it to the protection of a sandbagged bunker. But when he saw that a friend caught in the open fire had been seriously injured and was unable to get to cover under his own power, Earl ran through a barrage of exploding rounds to help. Before he could carry his wounded friend to safety, an exploding round mortally wounded him. He died a short time later.

In the Bible, John 15:13 says: *"Greater love has no man than this, that he lay down his life for his friends."*

My brother died carrying a friend, not firing a gun. He laid down his life for a friend he knew less than two years.

He is a hero. I honor him for his great love.

EARL WATSON THARP JR. is honored on Panel 9W, Row 97 of the Vietnam Veterans Memorial. He was awarded the Silver Star, Bronze Star, Air Medal (twice) and the Purple Heart.

JANE (THARP) WOODRUFF lived in Cape Girardeau, Mo., at the time of her brother's death. She and her husband now live in Virginia, where she home-schools her three children, is active in her church and is a foster parent for an adoption agency. In 2008, she joined VVMF's Teach Vietnam Teachers Network. One of her dreams is to travel to Vietnam and visit orphanages there.

Bob Cupp:
A Son and Brother
By
Emogene Cupp and Sue Rampey

Cpl. Robert William Cupp, son of James Russell Cupp and Emogene Moore Cupp, was born June 17, 1947 in Alexandria, Va.

Bob attended Bush Hill Elementary School, Mark Twain Middle School and Edison High School. He loved baseball and would throw the ball against our brick house and catch it. There were two large picture windows on the second floor of the house. He must have pitched that baseball thousands of times against the house between those windows and never broke a window! Every year that he was eligible, he played Little League Baseball and was fortunate enough always to be on the winning team.

He was drafted into the Army on August 24, 1967, and after receiving his basic training and his advanced training, he was shipped to Ft. Lewis, Wash., for deployment to Vietnam.

Bob's leave at Christmastime 1967 was a surprise to his family. We were so happy to see him, not realizing that it would be our last Christmas together.

We took him to Dulles Airport in February 1968 for his flight to Ft. Lewis and from there, he went on to Vietnam. Paul Copeland, an Army buddy he had gone all through training with, said he and Bob sat side by side on the flight to Vietnam. When the two arrived, they were put in different units. When their units crossed paths again, Paul learned that Bob lost his life when he stepped on a land mine.

There is no other feeling like opening your door to a knock and there stands a military man; you know it is bad news. He told us that Bob had been killed instantly on June 6, 1968 when he stepped on a land mine. The funeral was held on his 21st birthday.

Bob's friend from their school days, Steve Davenport, has always kept Bob in his heart. He sent roses to Bob's funeral, remembering the pact the two made: that whoever died first, the other would send roses. Steve also made one of Mrs. Cupp's favorite possessions. It is a beautiful 25-inch by 25-inch black lacquer display box containing the medals Bob earned, his picture and his name etched in the glass from a rubbing on The Wall. He made a duplicate and placed it at The Wall, and it is now in the Vietnam Veterans Memorial Collection of items that have been left at The Wall.

Bob's mother was pleased to be able to go to Vietnam in August 2002 and see where Bob was killed. Thanks to the veterans of the Dusters, Quads & Searchlight Organization for making the trip possible. Susan and Bob Lauver, Mike Sweeney and Greg Dearborn were great caring individuals to accompany the mothers and have so much compassion for them. Vietnam is a beautiful country, just like Bob said in his letters.

Jim, Bob's father, died on June 26, 1990. His parents, with scars on their hearts, will always remember their loving son, Robert William Cupp.

ROBERT WILLIAM CUPP is honored on Panel 60W, Row 27 of the Vietnam Veterans Memorial.

This article was written by his mother, EMOGENE M. CUPP, and his sister, SUE A. RAMPEY, both of whom regularly attend ceremonies at The Wall and are involved in other VVMF programs.

Shortly after Bob was killed, a member of the Alexandria Chapter of the American Gold Star Mothers asked Mrs. Cupp to join. She became active in the organization and was elected National President in 1978.

She met Jan Scruggs when he and Bob Doubek, also from VVMF, visited the Gold Star Mothers National Headquarters in Washington, D.C. looking for office space from which to lead the fight for a national memorial to those who served in Vietnam. They left without office space, but they gained the support of Mrs. Cupp, who volunteered to help in any way she could. A dedicated supporter from the beginning, Mrs. Cupp was a speaker at the groundbreaking ceremony and unveiled the first panel.

A True Soldier
By
Rachel Bunn Clinkscale

All of his life, my husband James A. Bunn wanted to be a soldier. His Uncle Howard Royal died while serving in World War II, and he was Jim's hero.

Even when he was a little boy, Jim was a leader and a protector. I recall when he was 6 and I was 5, we were playing in the park with some other children, one of whom stepped on a piece of glass and was bleeding. Jim picked her up and ran several blocks home with her to get help.

When Jim was 17, his mother signed for him to enter the Army. He served in Korea near the end of the conflict. When he came home, we were married.

He said to me, "If there is ever a war, I'll be one of the first to volunteer to go."

He served his first tour in Vietnam with the 101st Airborne from 1965-1966. After he came home, we were stationed at Ft. Campbell, Ky., where he was an instructor at the airborne jump school. He had been back less than a year when he came home and said the 3/506 was being reactivated, and he was going with them. He thought his experience might help to keep some of the young soldiers alive that were being sent to Vietnam. Jim died Feb. 2, 1968, trying to rescue one of those young soldiers.

Years later, I heard from several of those young men who described what happened and how Jim died. Jim was the platoon sergeant for Company A of the 3/506 and following are some of the comments made by those who served with him:

"Platoon Sgt. James Bunn has rarely ever been far from my mind. He was a good man and brave, and all of those things that we admire about exceptionally honorable people. I never worried about anything because I knew Jim Bunn had my back covered, and he did."
—*Lt. John Harrison*

"Vaughn [DeWaay] was there when Jim was hit and returned to bring him out. He loved Jim so much, he was the one person he would talk about. He called Jim his 'father figure' and said there wasn't a time that Jim wouldn't sit and listen when he needed to talk to someone."
—*Catherine DeWaay, wife of Vaugh DeWaay*

"Platoon Sgt. Bunn was our mentor and hero. His men respected him very much and would follow him 'to hell and back.'"
—*Jerry Berry*

"The day after Jim was KIA [killed in action], I helped evacuate him on the chopper, at which time I put my hand on him and gave him my 'Aloha.' Throughout all these years, I have thought about that day. As platoon sergeants, we tried to watch over the men as much as possible. Jim was much more experienced and made me feel confident that I also would do a good job. I feel I owe him a great deal."
—*Joe Jerviss (Pineapple)*

My husband was a true soldier who died for what he believed in. Not many of us can say that or be remembered this way. All of the names on The Wall represent individuals who were and are our true heroes.

JAMES ALBERT BUNN is honored on Panel 36E, Row 66 of the Vietnam Veterans Memorial.

RACHEL BUNN CLINKSCALE lives in Vincent, Ala. She is active with the Gold Star Wives of America, Inc., serving on the group's board of directors and chairing two committees. Gold Star Wives of America is a national military widows service organization chartered by the United States Congress.

They Were Our Friends

A Spirit that Does Not Compromise
By
Michael Heisley

I first met Rocky Versace when we were young boys growing up in Alexandria, Va., in 1950. As young boys, we had arguments and even a few fights. Rocky always maintained his opinion and never relented.

Over the years, from grade school through high school and college, our friendship matured and grew stronger. After graduation from college— Georgetown for me and West Point for Rocky—we corresponded by mail and telephone.

Rocky was posted first in the United States, then in South Korea. Later, he served two tours in Vietnam, back when the U.S. troops were primarily advisors.

On Rocky's last night of leave before returning to Vietnam to complete his second tour of duty, he dined with me and my wife Agnes in our home. At dinner, Rocky informed us he was leaving the service after his second tour. He planned to become a priest in the Maryknoll Order and stay in Vietnam to work with orphanages for the children of Vietnam, whom he deeply loved. I promised to help him with his dream.

We parted, never to see each other again.

Months later, while living in Dallas, Texas, my wife and I learned from a television news report that Capt. Rocky Versace had been wounded and captured by the Viet Cong on Oct. 29, 1963. I will never forget that evening. I told Agnes, "I fear we will never see Rocky again. Rocky has a spirit that does not compromise. He will not bend or break. They will have to kill him."

Over the next several years, Agnes and I prayed for his release and waited for news about Rocky. From time to time, we got vague reports about the Viet Cong marching him from village to village for propaganda purposes.

Finally, our worst fears were realized when we learned that Rocky had been executed on Sept. 26, 1965.

Rocky's belief in God, his love of his country and his commitment to West Point's code of Duty, Honor and Country had finally convinced his captors that they could not break him—they could only kill him.

Almost 40 years later, on a sunny day in Alexandria, Va., the Captain Rocky Versace Plaza and Vietnam Veterans Memorial was dedicated to the people of Alexandria who had died in Vietnam. At the center of the memorial is a statue of Rocky with his arms around two Vietnamese children.

Later that weekend, at a White House ceremony on July 8, 2002, my wife and I watched as President George W. Bush awarded the Congressional Medal of Honor posthumously to our friend Rocky. It was the first time an Army POW had been awarded the nation's highest honor for actions in captivity.

I felt that, although his body was never recovered and still rested in some unknown, dark jungle clearing in the Mekong Delta, his spirit was at last home in Arlington National Cemetery, where a gravestone had been placed for him.

I erected a duplicate of Rocky's Alexandria Vietnam Veterans Memorial statue in front of my home in St. Charles, Ill. It has the American flag flanked by the

POW/MIA flag and the West Point flag. It is a symbol for me and all who visit my home. And, it is a tribute to Rocky and the men and women who gave their lives in service to their country. Every day, it reminds me of Rocky.

No day passes that I don't look at that memorial and remember the man, the patriot and my great friend.

HUMBERT ROQUE VERSACE is honored on Panel 1E, Row 33 of the Vietnam Veterans Memorial.

MICHAEL HEISLEY is the owner of the Memphis Grizzlies, and is a Chicago businessman involved in multiple business ventures. His family charitable foundation, the Heisley Family Foundation, is deeply involved in children's charities and is a strong supporter of St. Jude's Children's Hospital. The Heisley Family Foundation also supports the Education Center at The Wall.

My Silent Partner
By
Barbara L. Smith

Bob Farrington was my fiancé. We became engaged before he left for Vietnam, where he was a scout helicopter pilot. He loved flying. He loved adventure. He loved life. Yet, three months after reporting to Vietnam, he was dead. Bob was 24 years old; I was 26.

Bob was the sole surviving son of his family. His parents were dead, and he was raised by his grandmother. He was a wonderful man—sensitive to the needs of others, but with a funny streak that could keep you laughing for hours. We met on Easter eve 1968, and we spent many hours investigating the areas surrounding where he was stationed at Fort Sill in Oklahoma, either on his motorcycle or in his new Mustang convertible.

But, since I was not family, I did not receive information about how he died. And, for 30 years, I lived with the questions: Did he suffer? Or did he die quickly?

I lost Bob on Dec. 11, 1969. In June 1999, almost 30 years later, I visited *The Wall That Heals*, a half-size replica of the Vietnam Veterans Memorial, when it traveled to Mansfield, Pa. There, I met John Anderson, *The Wall That Heals* site manager. When I asked him if he could use the computers in the information area to give me information about Bob, he became very excited and said, "He was a Blue Ghost!" I did not know what he was talking about, but quickly learned that John was a medic in Bob's unit, the Blue Ghosts.

John hooked me up with those wonderful veterans who served with Bob. Soon my questions were answered. The members of the Blue Ghosts saved my life and helped me move on.

From that encounter in Pennsylvania, I decided I wanted to help people the way I had been helped. I wanted to help them find information, reconnect and remember those lost in Vietnam.

When John and his wife Linda retired in 2005, I became one of the site managers for *The Wall That Heals*. I had gotten my commercial driver's license and learned to drive a truck, which was challenging, several years before. But the rest of the work, helping people and teaching them about Vietnam, was easy. My previous job had been as an adult educator and manager.

As I brought *The Wall That Heals* to communities throughout the United States and Canada, I felt as if Bob were traveling with me, as a silent partner in my mission to help people remember and heal.

We were a great team. Bob's name was on The Wall, helping young and old remember that each name represented a loving member of a family, a friend, a buddy, a lover, a neighbor. I drove the truck, set up The Wall, set up the tent, trained the volunteers, collected donations, wrote reports and helped people find their special names on The Wall. Even when they thought it would be impossible to find the name, because they had so little information and maybe only a nickname, I was patient and persistent and was able to find many names for people. We were helping people reconnect and remember in our own way.

Throughout the four years that I was site manager, I always left yellow roses at the panel containing Bob's name. We had given each other yellow roses while we were dating, and it was a symbol of our love. At each stop, I would approach The Wall, touch his name and say, "Here we go again." Even after 40 years, we were working together as a team.

As I write this essay, I have a bouquet of yellow roses on my desk, reminding me of one man who died to give me freedom.

ROBERT DEAN FARRINGTON is honored on Panel 15W, Row 48 of the Vietnam Veterans Memorial.

BARBARA L. SMITH lives in Arroyo Grande, Calif. She was the site manager for The Wall That Heals from 2005-2009

They Inspire Us

Honoring the Grandfather I Never Met
By
Megan Rihn

Ever since I can remember, I have been traveling to the Vietnam Veterans Memorial with my family to honor my grandfather, SP4 Joel D. Coleman, who was killed in action in Vietnam in May of 1966.

My mother was a baby when he died, so neither of us ever knew him. But the stories my grandmother tells about him have been an important part of our family tradition.

I like the story about the day my mom was born. The Army was not going to allow my grandfather to come home to Pittsburgh to see my mom. He did everything he could to get there, but they would not allow it. My 4'11" great-grandmother then decided to take on the U.S. Army and get him home to see his newborn daughter. As it turns out, she got her way! My grandfather showed up at the hospital with flowers and surprised my grandmother. Everyone knew that he was coming home except my grandmother. She was thrilled.

My grandfather had to leave for Vietnam on Dec. 22, 1965. My mom was only two and a half months old. His leaving was very difficult, but being three days before Christmas made it even worse. He gave my grandmother a gold watch that year—little did she know that it would be the last gift he would ever give her.

The night my family took him to the airport, he told my grandmother that the Army was sending him someplace safe. He didn't want her to worry, but she knew better. Vietnam was a very dangerous place. His leaving put a hole in her heart. She had a feeling that she would never see him again and that she would be left to raise my mom alone.

My grandmother wrote to my grandfather every day and sometimes sent him care packages. In his letters, he would tell her how things were going with him and his unit, but never anything that would make her worry. But once again, she knew better.

My grandfather also sent letters to family and friends. Only from these letters did she know how terrible things really were for him. He would spend many weeks away from camp, living in foxholes and getting very little sleep. He would jump out of helicopters behind enemy lines and come into close combat with the North Vietnamese Army. He sent several pictures of himself and his buddies enjoying the care packages sent from home. The pictures show that life there was rough, but he and his buddies still had some good times together.

My grandmother described to me the night my grandfather died. The night before she received the telegram from the Army, she took my mom out to buy her first pair of shoes. It was May 5, 1966. She told me that when they were shopping, she noticed the strongest aroma of roses, at approximately 6:30 p.m. The following day, an officer and chaplain sent by the Army arrived at her house to tell her that my grandfather had been killed at 6:30 p.m. the day before. He was so young, only 21 years old.

My family remembers and honors my grandfather at the Vietnam Veterans Memorial. Attending Memorial Day, Veterans Day and a few Father's Day ceremonies, as well as volunteering at The Wall, have been a huge part of my life over the past 18 years.

I have learned a lot about the Vietnam War and The Wall from those visits, and I have also learned a lot from doing multiple school projects about the Memorial and what it means to my family.

In fifth grade, I was given an assignment to interview someone about a major event in his or her life and write a book about it. As a curious 10-year-old who had grown up hearing stories about my grandfather, I chose to interview my grandmother, Susan Coleman, about when my grandfather received his orders for Vietnam. My book was picked out of 150 submitted and put in our middle school's library. Four copies of the book were printed and bound: one for my school, one for my grandmother, one for my mom and one to leave at The Wall.

I also chose to incorporate the Vietnam Veterans Memorial into my high school graduation project. I decided to raise money for the Education Center at The Wall, which will be a place to tell the stories and put faces to the names of the many men and women whose names are inscribed on the Vietnam Veterans Memorial.

I wrote a letter asking for donations and sent it to veterans' organizations around the Pittsburgh area, as well as a few others nationally. I also collected donations at my high school. Overall, I raised $1,078—more than double my original goal.

This project was special to me because of my family's connection to The Wall. It is important to me that my grandfather is remembered and his story is told, as well as the stories of the more than 58,000 other service members whose names are on The Wall.

I know that, as time goes on, I will continue learning about my grandfather's life. And someday, I will tell those stories to my children and visit The Wall with them, just as my mom and grandmother did with me. My grandfather will always be a hero to my family, and we will never forget him.

JOEL DANIEL COLEMAN is honored on Panel 7E, Row 29 of the Vietnam Veterans Memorial.

MEGAN RIHN is a senior at Shaler Area High School near Pittsburgh, Pa. She is part of three generations of women—including her grandmother, mother and younger sister—dedicated to ensuring that the lives and stories of those whose names are on The Wall are not forgotten.

Learning About a Hometown Hero
By
McKenzie Mathewson
and
Shannon Kievit

The National Call for Photos—Put A Face With A Name—Our "Hometown Hero." Our history teacher thought it would be a great project for us to research the person from our town whose name is on the Vietnam Veterans Memorial. She thought it could be tied into our annual Veterans Day commemoration. As she described the project, we were intrigued. It sounded like an easy report.

We had no idea the impact Michael Jonas Pynnonen would have on our lives.

Who was this young man who died over 40 years ago? Research began with the last years of Mike's life. His high school yearbook gave us pictures. Our teacher knew his cousin and his sister. They, in turn, gave us the names of Mike's high school buddies, who shared stories of Mike's life as he grew up in Lewiston, Mich. They shared stories about his days as a football and basketball star. The girls remembered that Mike was so handsome.

Talking with his sister was an extremely moving experience for us. We found out that his death was incredibly hard on her, and even to this day, she hasn't been able to make a visit to The Wall. Something that happened decades ago still affects her greatly.

We discovered something neither of us had expected:

The names on The Wall had faces. The faces became real people for us. The emotional impact of this research was overwhelming.

When we began the project, our hometown hero was someone unknown to us, but we came to feel sadness for such a loss, compassion for his family and friends, and gratitude for his service to our country.

A trip to Washington, D.C., gave us the opportunity to visit The Wall. There was Mike's name. We were moved to tears. Seeing all of those names was a heart-wrenching experience.

All of those people's names made us think about what they sacrificed. They all had hopes, dreams and families. So many of their own personal hopes and dreams never came true.

As for their families, they were crushed when the news came about the death of their loved ones. We can only imagine the pain caused by losing someone so tragically. It was awful to think of all the wives who would never see their husbands again; children growing up without fathers; and the mothers and fathers who lost their children. Sitting there at The Wall made us think about all the emotions attached to that wall of names. The thought of putting a face with every name seemed very appropriate.

In the past, we had not always had an interest in history. Then, we realized that the stories of the people whose names are on The Wall *are* our history. It struck us that history really is important. Now, it is not just a book that spits facts at us; history is alive. Today, we are honored to be learning about the things that happened in the past.

Without that emotional experience of learning about Michael Pynnonen and seeing all of those names on The Wall, we wouldn't have been able to connect with history as we do today. Through this whole experience, we have learned many values and the importance of our country.

By speaking with groups in our community, we hope we have inspired others to find out how they can help build the Education Center at The Wall. More importantly, we hope that other students will honor their hometown heroes by researching their lives. It will make history come alive for them, too.

By working on this project, we have developed a new appreciation for our country, realizing the price of freedom.

Our hearts have been touched. Our minds have been opened to the past.

MICHAEL JONAS PYNNONEN is honored on Panel 12W, Row 58 of the Vietnam Veterans Memorial.

MCKENZIE MATHEWSON and SHANNON KIEVIT are eighth graders at Lewiston Middle School in Lewiston, Mich. They researched Michael Jonas Pynnonen for a school project and presented his photograph at the launch of VVMF's National Call for Photos in September 2009. Mathewson and Kievit traveled to Washington, D.C. for the event, spoke about their hometown hero and were interviewed by members of the media about their research.

Remembering 612 Connecticut Heroes
By
Tom Dzicek

As part of a school-wide enrichment program at Capt. Nathan Hale Middle School, I would ask local veterans to come and talk about their experiences. Small groups of students interviewed these veterans of World War II, Korea and Vietnam. The students were in absolute awe of the men and women who came in and not only spoke to them, but also brought a variety of war souvenirs. The students documented the interviews and compiled them into a book. The impact of presenting the book to the interviewed veterans was a truly moving experience.

History was coming alive for the students!

As part of those initial interviews, we discovered that two men from our small town of Coventry, Conn., were killed in Vietnam.

My students asked how many U.S. service personnel were killed in Vietnam; I was able to respond that it was 58,220. [At the time, this is how many names were on the Vietnam Veterans Memorial. This number changes as names are added to The Wall.]

How many, they asked, were from Connecticut? I didn't know. A little research allowed me to answer that question the next day: 612 men from Connecticut died in the Vietnam War. The students wanted to know more about the men, many of whom were not much older than they are now. What transpired as a result of this student curiosity had, and continues to have, an impact on the students, the town and the state of Connecticut.

After enlisting the support of staff and talking with students, we began the quest to learn more. There are 612 names of Connecticut servicemen on the Vietnam Veterans Memorial in Washington, D.C. Our project was to research each name and compile the information into a book.

Much information was readily available on the Internet. Students also contacted every newspaper, radio station and television station in the state. Many responses from family members, service buddies, veterans' organizations and childhood friends were also used as we compiled information.

Simultaneously, reading and social studies cross-curriculum projects dealing with the Vietnam War were being conducted. In addition, an artistic portrayal of all 612 names was being placed on a wall near our new school auditorium. The artistic portrayal is a black map of Connecticut measuring 13 feet by 9 feet. Within this map are painted all 612 names of the Connecticut men who were lost in Vietnam, arranged by year of death, then alphabetically.

We coordinated with the Vietnam Veterans Memorial Fund in Washington, D.C. to host the half-scale traveling replica of The Wall, called *The Wall That Heals*, in May 2002. During the exhibition, the rough drafts of the 612 veterans' biographies were available for visitors to read and add more information. Students were also available for on-the-spot interviews and further data collection. They also served as guides for visitors to the traveling replica, putting special emphasis on the 612 names from Connecticut.

Also, as part of the exhibition, students researched and displayed trivia cards dealing with life in the 1960s and 1970s. Display cases located across from the auditorium exhibited artifacts from the era and housed items on loan from people who wanted to share possessions from brothers, fathers and husbands who were killed or who had served in Vietnam.

To the best of our knowledge, nothing like this had been done before. As the project unfolded, we became aware that it would be the only place in the state where all the names of the Connecticut men lost in Vietnam were in one place available for public viewing.

The project involved students from all grade levels, 6-8, who wrote, revised and edited biographical sketches; painted murals of scenes that related to the conflict; researched and developed trivia cards about the era; read about *The Wall That Heals*; and participated in units of study about the Vietnam conflict and the Vietnam era.

Personal interviews, radio interviews and phone interviews with friends and family members of the 612 servicemen provided insight and a personal touch to many of their stories.

The first four books "off the press" were placed at the Vietnam Veterans Memorial on Veterans Day 2002, which was also the 20th anniversary of The Wall. Jan Scruggs, founder and president of VVMF, personally accepted copies of the book on behalf of his organization.

Copies were also given to families of the fallen veterans as part of a student-conducted "Project Reflection" program, and a copy was mailed to every town in the state of Connecticut and to the Connecticut State Library.

Jean Risely of Coventry, Conn., was inspired by the 612 Project. Her brother, Robert Tillquist, was a combat medic and Distinguished Service Cross recipient who died in the Pleiku Campaign in Vietnam on Nov. 4, 1965. She wanted to create a memorial to honor her brother and all of the 612 Connecticut men, to thank them and to welcome them home.

Risely formed a group called the Connecticut Vietnam Veterans Memorial Committee to raise money for the memorial and see it through to completion. Fundraising began in earnest in 2006; ground was broken in 2007; and the Connecticut Vietnam Veterans Memorial was dedicated on May 17, 2008.

TOM DZICEK is a veteran and a teacher at Nathan Hale Middle School in Coventry, Conn. He is a member of VVMF's Teach Vietnam Teachers Network, where educators at all grade levels share resources and ideas about teaching the Vietnam War in the classroom, and a member of the Advisory Board for the Education Center at The Wall.

For more information about the Connecticut Vietnam Veterans Memorial, visit www.cvvm.org.

With Dreams to Pursue:
Remembering Two Young Men
By
James Wright

I grew up in a mining town, Galena, Ill. With four friends, I joined the Marines in 1957 at the age of 17—to keep me out of the mines for at least a few years. When I returned in 1960, I decided to go to college— but I needed to work in the mines while in school. My boss when I worked underground was Clarence Lyden. He was a good boss, a good man, who had received a Purple Heart while serving in the Army in World War II. He encouraged me to become a powderman, set- ting dynamite charges, in order to earn 20 cents more an hour. I did take on this assignment and continued to study—and was a student teacher back in my old high school.

One of my students in an English class was Clarence Lyden's son, Michael. I remember him as an energetic, pleasant, hard-working young man. A few years later, he was drafted and went into the Army, where he became a sergeant in the 101st Airborne. Already hold- ing a Purple Heart, Michael died on May 15, 1969 in Operation Apache Snow at a place we remember as Hamburger Hill.

The Wall records the sons—and daughters—of many miners, factory workers, farmers and so many others. The Wall contains the names of 15 graduates of Dartmouth College. I did not know any of them. But

I came to know well the father, the sister, the brother, the classmates, the coach and teammates of one.

Bill Smoyer grew up in comfortable circumstances in New Jersey. At Dartmouth, he was an All-Ivy soccer player and a star hockey player. He was by all accounts a gracious and generous young man, a gentleman. And he joined the Marines in order to go to Vietnam because he believed that wars should not be fought only by the sons of the miners, farmers and factory workers. He was in Vietnam for only two weeks on July 28, 1968 when his platoon was caught in an ambush while crossing a rice paddy at An Hoa. 2nd Lt. Smoyer and 18 other members of Kilo company, 3rd Battalion Seventh Marines were killed that Sunday.

Who knows what Billy Smoyer and Mike Lyden would have done with their lives? Mike may have gone back to work at the Kraft Foods plant in Galena—he did not want to follow his dad into the mines. His old teacher here believes that whatever he did, he would have done well. Billy Smoyer was a history major who may have gone into business—but all attest that whatever he did, he would have tried to make a difference for others.

In the summer of 2009, my wife, Susan, and I visited Normandy, where we spent a lot of time walking through the American cemetery at Colleville. The white marble crosses and Stars of David filled the hillside with a sense of order and tranquility—and whispered of lives lost. We walked among the graves for some time, reading the names, observing where they were from and how old they were. We thought of lives cut short and of dreams unrealized and wanted to know more about them.

Casualties of war cry out to be known — as persons, not as abstractions called "casualties" nor as numbers entered into the books, and not only as names chiseled into marble or granite. We have carried in our memories the stories of those recorded here, but memories fade, as do those who remember. We are graying. After all of us who knew them are gone, the names on The Wall will endure.

It is essential that the Education Center planned for a site near The Wall sparkle with the human records of those whose sacrifice was forever. We need to ensure that here, in this place of memory, lives as well as names are recorded — lives with smiling human faces, remarkable accomplishments, engaging personalities and with dreams to pursue. We do this for them, for history and for those in the future who will send the young to war.

MICHAEL P. LYDEN is honored on Panel 24W, Row 18 of the Vietnam Veterans Memorial.

WILLIAM STANLEY SMOYER is honored on Panel 50W, Row 28 of the Vietnam Veterans Memorial.

JAMES WRIGHT is president emeritus at Dartmouth College in Hanover, N. H. This story is adapted from remarks he made at The Wall on Veterans Day 2009.

Never Stop Trying
By
Jan C. Scruggs

All of us have had the experience of wanting something so badly and then not achieving it. As we are taught from our youth, most of us pick ourselves up, dust ourselves off and try again.

This reaction is not always instantaneous. Some might need time to nurse bruised egos or lick their wounds—but not Clifton Cushman.

This extraordinary young man from Grand Forks, N.D., had known incredible success and heart-wrenching failure in his young life. He won a silver medal in the 1960 Olympic games in Rome in the 400-meter hurdles.

In 1964, while competing in the Olympic trials in Los Angeles to earn a spot on the American Olympic team, he hit a hurdle during the race and fell, eliminating himself from the competition.

We can only imagine how crushing this disappointment was to the one-time Olympian. But instead of sulking, Cushman wrote a remarkably upbeat letter to the young people of his home town, encouraging them to set goals for themselves. At the time, the letter was printed in the *Grand Forks Herald* on the front page and has been reprinted nationally many times since then.

He did very well in sports at the University of Kansas and, after graduation, joined the U.S. Air Force and was stationed in Vietnam.

On Sept. 25, 1966, he was conducting an afternoon combat mission to bomb a railroad bridge located on the northeast railroad line approximately one mile north-northeast of Kep MiG base and 29 miles northeast of Bac Giang, Lang Son Province, North Vietnam. His plane was hit by anti-aircraft artillery fire and broke into several pieces. Observers saw his seat eject from the wreckage, but his body was not found. He was declared dead in 1975.

It has been many years since Cliff Cushman set athletic records in his hometown, but the people of Grand Forks have not forgotten him. Grand Forks Central High School named its football stadium after him, and some of his high school athletic records have stood for 50 years.

In 1997, the Cushman Classic was inaugurated, a high school football match up between Grand Forks Central and Red River High Schools. Most local athletes have heard the letter, and it is read annually before the kickoff of this event.

The letter is reprinted here. All these years later, it still has the power to inspire. After all he had been through, Cliff Cushman sought to use his experience to help other young people. Knowing what was in store for him and how his life would end in service to his country just a few short years later makes this hero seem even more remarkable and selfless.

To The Youth of Grand Forks . . .

Don't feel sorry for me. I feel sorry for some of you! You may have seen the U.S. Olympic Trials on televi-

sion September 13. If so, you watched me hit the fifth hurdle, fall and lie on the track in an inglorious heap of skinned elbows, bruised hips, torn knees, and injured pride, unsuccessful in my attempt to make the Olympic team for the second time. In a split second all the many years of training, pain, sweat, blisters, and agony of running were simply and irrevocably wiped out. But I tried. I would much rather fail knowing I had put forth an honest effort than never have tried at all.

This is not to say that everyone is capable of making the Olympic Team. However, each of you is capable of trying to make your own personal "Olympic Team," whether it be the high school football team, the glee club, the honor roll, or whatever your goal may be. Unless your reach exceeds your grasp, how can you be sure what you can attain? And don't you think there are things better than cigarettes, hot-rod cars, school drop-outs, excessive make-up, and ducktail grease-cuts?

Over fifteen years ago I saw a star-first place in the Olympic Games. I literally started to run after it. In 1960 I came within three yards of grabbing it; this year I stumbled, fell and watched it recede four more years away. Certainly, I was very disappointed in falling flat on my face. However, there is nothing I can do about it now but get up, pick the cinders from my wounds, and take one more step, followed by one more and one more, until the steps turn into miles and the miles into success.

I know I may never make it. The odds are against me but I have something in my favor-desire and faith. Romans 5:3-5 has always had an inspirational meaning to me in this regard, "...we rejoice in our suffer-

ings, knowing that suffering produces endurance, and endurance produces character, and character produces hope, and hope does not disappoint us..." At least I am going to try.

How about you? Would a little extra effort on your part bring up you grade average? Would you have a better chance to make the football team if you stayed an extra 15 minutes after practice and worked on your blocking?

Let me tell you something about yourselves. You are taller and heavier than any past generation in this country. You are spending more money, enjoying more freedom, and driving more cars than ever before, yet many of you are very unhappy. Some of you have never known the satisfaction of doing your best in sports, the joy of excelling in class, the wonderful feeling of completing a job, any job, and looking back on it knowing that you have done your best.

I dare you to have your hair cut and not wilt under the comments of your so-called friends. I dare you to clean up your language. I dare you to honor your mother and father. I dare you to go to church without having to be compelled to go by your parents. I dare you to unselfishly help someone less fortunate than yourself and enjoy the wonderful feeling that goes with it. I dare you to become physically fit. I dare you to read a book that is not required in school. I dare you to look up at the stars, not down at the mud, and set your sights on one of them that, up to now, you thought was unattainable. There is plenty of room at the top, but no room for anyone to sit down.

Who knows? You may be surprised at what you can

achieve with sincere effort. So get up, pick the cinders out of your wounds, and take one more step.

I dare you!

CLIFTON EMMET CUSHMAN is honored on Panel 11E, Row 13 of the Vietnam Veterans Memorial.

JAN C. SCRUGGS is the founder and president of the Vietnam Veterans Memorial Fund. He is a wounded and decorated veteran of the Vietnam War, having served in the 199th Light Infantry Brigade of the U.S. Army.

We Lost Them Later

An Old Man's Folly
By
Adm. Elmo R. Zumwalt Jr.

As part of the Veteran's Day festivities in 1992, I was asked to lay a wreath at the recently completed U.S. Navy Memorial in Washington, D.C. Included in this memorial, along with a statue of the "Lone Sailor," are a series of bronze bas reliefs, each depicting a different era in our naval history. I laid the commemorative wreath at the foot of the bronze relief dedicated to the "Brown Water Navy," the name given to those who served on the small boats operating in the narrow waterways of Vietnam during that conflict.

The ceremony was an emotional one for me, for two reasons. First, I had commanded for two years those sailors who had so valiantly served in the Brown Water Navy. Second, the scene depicted was of Swift Boat #35—the boat commanded by my older son, Elmo, who had served under my command at that time.

While Elmo survived the fighting in Vietnam, he failed to survive the war. Despite a courageous five-year struggle, he eventually succumbed to cancer believed to have been caused by his exposure to Agent Orange, the chemical defoliant used—on my direct orders—to deny the Viet Cong the concealment provided by the heavily vegetated riverbeds.

That Veteran's Day was also the 10th anniversary of the Vietnam Veterans Memorial. Despite its stark simplicity, The Wall cannot help but cause the observer—whether or not he or she ever served in uniform—to be moved. Focusing on a single name there makes one ponder how and where that particular individual met death. Was it painful and protracted or mercifully swift? What were this person's last thoughts? What personal legacy has survived?

A painting of The Wall by Lee Teter perhaps best sums up some of the common emotions evoked by viewing this awesome memorial:

The scene appears to take place on a pleasantly warm autumn day. A man wearing a three-piece suit, his sleeves rolled up, with his suit jacket draped over his briefcase on the ground next to him, stands with his left hand in his pocket, leaning with his right hand above his head against The Wall. The touch of gray in the man's neatly trimmed beard suggests he is in his 50s. His head is bowed; his eyes are tightly shut; he is immersed in deep reflection—perhaps about a fallen comrade, brother or father.

While the observer can only guess at the reason for this man's particular grief, the artist has left no doubt that the experience for this visitor to The Wall is a painfully emotional one. At the point where the visitor's right hand comes in contact with The Wall, one can see an outstretched hand—emanating from within the Memorial—pressed firmly against the grieving man's hand, as if the two were separated only by a pane of glass. The arm leads to the ghostlike figure of a young helmeted soldier, still in battle camouflaged uniform, peering out at the bereaved visitor, who is oblivious to the soldier's presence. The soldier, perhaps the dead friend or relative about whom the visitor is reflecting, is flanked on either side by similar apparitions in varied degrees of battlefield uniform. The apparition to the immediate left of the soldier with the outstretched arm has his right hand on that soldier's shoulder, as if to comfort the soldier who is anguishing, in turn, over the grief exhibited by the visitor. These spirits, unable to reach out to the visitor, their voices silent forever, convey in their faces the message clearly locked in their hearts: "Do not grieve for us, dear friend, for we are finally at peace."

The Teter print is appropriately titled, "Reflections."

Perhaps it is just an old man's folly, but now when I visit the Vietnam Veterans Memorial, I pause to press my hand firmly against the black granite wall. I then envision Elmo's hand reaching out to touch mine. And in a plea that will forever remain silent in this world, I see in his eyes the message he is trying to convey from his heart: "Do not grieve for me, Dad, for I am finally at peace."

ELMO RUSSELL ZUMWALT III died on Aug. 13, 1988, from cancer related to Agent Orange exposure. He is one of nearly 2,000 individuals who have been honored through VVMF's In Memory program.

ADM. ELMO ZUMWALT JR. spoke at the first In Memory Day ceremony in 1999, when his son was added to the In Memory Honor Roll. Adm. Zumwalt died on Jan. 2, 2000. This essay is adapted from an article he wrote in 1993, a year after attending the 10th anniversary ceremony at The Wall and laying the wreath at the new U.S. Navy Memorial in Washington, D.C., and is printed with permission from his son, James Zumwalt.

A Lifelong Dream of Flight
By
Patricia Kelly

Vincent J. Kelly was born Sept. 30, 1937 in Buffalo, N.Y., to Leo and Estella (Graff) Kelly. He was the second of six children.

During his youth, his dream was to become a pilot, so his father would take him to watch planes flying in and out of the Buffalo Airport. Vince graduated from high school and enlisted in the U.S. Air Force in June 1955, where he became a jet aircraft mechanic. When he was discharged in 1959, he applied for and was accepted into the cadet pilot training program at Reese Air Force Base in Texas.

Vince and I met at a wedding in Phoenix, Ariz., when one of his classmates married a friend of mine. Our courtship was long distance, as Vince was now stationed at Cannon Air Force Base in New Mexico, and I lived in Phoenix. We married in August 1963 during his leave between Cannon and his new assignment to the 48th Tactical Fighter Wing at RAF Lakenheath, England.

At first, his principal duty was as an alert officer. But in March 1964, he was assigned to the 493rd Squadron, and oh, was he happy! He could be a fighter pilot. He reveled in this job, as it was fulfilling his lifelong dream. He just wanted to fly, fly, fly! He was always happy when the squadron went to Wheelus (Libya), Aviano (Italy), Madrid (Spain) or anywhere that the good weather meant more flying.

I think his one unhappiness was that he didn't own a sports car anymore. He had sold his beloved 1963 Corvette Stingray before leaving the United States. Maybe that was a good thing, because he'd probably drive it like he flew his F-100. As it was, he drove our little Volkswagen Bug almost like a sports car.

Our life in England was good. We met many wonderful English people and took occasional trips to London and a tour to Ireland. In June 1966, when Vince had a temporary assignment as a forward air controller for the Army, we drove through Belgium and around Germany. Our daughters were born during that time, too, in 1964 and 1966.

The Vietnam conflict was heating up, and in March 1967, Vince was assigned as a fighter pilot to Phan Rang Air Force Base and to the 614th Tactical Fighter Squadron, "B" Flight. I think Vince's tour in Vietnam, which lasted from March 1967 to March 1968, must have been exhilarating for him. He earned the Silver Star, the Distinguished Flying Cross and the Air Medal with oak leaf clusters. He flew an F-100 Super Sabre jet in 340 combat missions, totaling 526 combat hours. All of this flying couldn't help but fulfill his boyhood dream.

Stateside, Vince was an instructor pilot at Luke Air Force Base in Arizona. As he was adjusting to this new job, he started feeling ill and was diagnosed with Hodgkin's disease, a cancer originating in the white blood cells that spreads through the lymph nodes. His condition was treated with chemotherapy, but as it progressed, he needed continuous chemotherapy and close medical follow-up. He retired in March 1969 because of what was considered a service-connected disability. After being in the U.S. Air Force for 12 years and flying over 2,000 hours, he was now given a new military classification: 4-F. He was crushed.

Vince fought the cancer valiantly, but on March 12, 1970, the Hodgkin's disease won. Capt. Vincent Kelly passed away while in the Veterans Hospital in Phoenix, Ariz. He left behind his wife and two daughters, loving parents, siblings and many close relatives and friends.

It wasn't until the late 1980s that I heard about Agent Orange and the health ramifications it had for Vietnam veterans. After submitting his medical records in 1994, I received notification that his Hodgkin's disease and subsequent death were attributed to Agent Orange exposure.

VINCENT J. KELLY died as a result of his service in Vietnam in 1970 and was installed in VVMF's In Memory Program in 2006. His name is among the nearly 2,000 that make up the In Memory Honor Roll, which pays tribute to those who died as a result of the Vietnam War, but who do not meet Department of Defense criteria to have their names added to The Wall.

PATRICIA C. KELLY lives in Phoenix, Ariz.

Eulogy for Chris Benedict
By
Ed Chavez

Years ago, Chris Benedict came into the Social Security office where I work and asked to see me. He looked very dashing in his suede jacket, cowboy hat and boots. At the time, I knew he had served in Vietnam and had service-connected injuries, but not until this interview did I realize the extent of his disabilities.

One of the items he needed to file a claim was a DD-214, to establish his record of active-duty service. Check. He was a Marine. "You went to Vietnam twice?" I asked.

He nodded. "I volunteered."

There was much more to Chris than he let on. He briefly described the loss of sight in his left eye, his reconstructive surgeries and his exposure to Agent Orange. More operations and tests were needed. Since we were related by marriage, I told him I had to disqualify myself, but we arranged for another representative to process his claim.

When he left the building with that confident stride of his, two young ladies working in the office came up and asked me about him: "So, who is the Sundance Kid?"

"That's my cousin's husband," I told them.

"He's married?" Their hopes were dashed.

Chris had many blessings. He had a magnetic, physical presence. He had immense personal charm. He was the kind of person who is genuinely interested in others.

His courage was heroic—not only in combat, which earned him two Bronze Stars and a Silver Star—but in the courage he showed us in his day-to-day living with pain and with the knowledge that his athletic prowess was limited by his injuries. By degrees and through the years, we witnessed how he had to stop hiking, fishing and golfing.

He taught his wife to fish and Lynda gamely kept right on, even after he could no longer wade the streams with her or cast a rod. Instead, he'd watch her at the riverside and then clean whatever she brought on her string. "She's the catcher and I'm the cleaner," is how he described it.

Of his many blessings, Lynda quite possibly was his greatest gift. Chris and Lynda took their wedding vows seriously: "For better or for worse, in sickness and in health, for richer or for poorer." Along with her personal beauty, Chris saw in Lynda a history of stability, a family that interacts with warmth and concern, an extended family that included parents, grandparents, sisters, brothers, nieces and nephews. Chris saw that human happiness does not happen. Rather, happiness is the result of daily effort.

The Bible teaches us that when we endure suffering, we should not put on a long face. Chris knew there was no merit in trying to elicit pity or praise. He did what he was supposed to do. He persevered. Chris was not a quitter. No one ever heard him complain or whine, "Why me?"

Chris was optimistic. The pessimist would say Chris had little reason to live. But Chris, the incurable optimist, saw only what there was to live for. His sweet tooth was enough! He was famous with his nieces and nephews who knew he was an easy touch for that pocketful of Smarties he always carried with him. And when you were in his kitchen, he pressed you to join him for a Haagen Dazs. More than that, he was loyal to his friends, he was eager to make new ones and he had only pleasant things to say about people and to people.

Chris was a strong and cheerful person who bore his burdens with optimism and patience. But how much blood does a soldier have to spill to be awarded the Purple Heart three times? His suffering did not end in Vietnam, either. To be afflicted by post-traumatic stress disorder, as he was when he returned home, one is doomed to relive the horror again and again at unexpected moments.

We don't have Chris to worry about anymore; there is no more pain for him. We should thank him for the priceless gifts he gave us: for his example of perseverance and courage; for his optimism that shouted, "Life, indeed, is worth living!" and for spending his life for us.

CHRIS BENEDICT died as a result of his service in Vietnam in 1997 and was among those honored in VVMF's first In Memory Ceremony on Memorial Day 1998. To date, nearly 2,000 men and women have been honored through the In Memory program.

ED CHAVEZ lives in Albuquerque, N.M. This story is adapted from the eulogy he gave at Chris Benedict's funeral in September 1997 and is printed with permission from Chris's wife Lynda Benedict, who travels to Washington, D.C. every year to participate in the In Memory program and who traveled to Vietnam with VVMF in 2010.

Salute to a Special Hero

The Man Who Predicted 9/11

Rick Rescorla is an American hero and a Vietnam veteran. His name is not on the Vietnam Veterans Memorial because he came home from that war, only to perish on a day when so many other Americans also died: Sept. 11, 2001.

On that day, 2,605 individuals in the World Trade Center's twin towers died when the buildings collapsed after airplanes had been flown into them by terrorist hijackers. But, because of the skill, preparedness and bravery of Rick Rescorla, nearly 2,700 employees of Morgan Stanley *did not* die that day.

The story of his successful rescue efforts on 9/11 actually started years earlier. Rescorla worked as head of security for Morgan Stanley, which had offices in the World Trade Center. In the early 1990s, he performed a security evaluation of the building and determined that the unguarded underground garage was a logical target for a terrorist truck bomb.

Rescorla brought his safety concerns to the Port Authority, which owned the World Trade Center, but his advice was ignored.

On Feb. 26, 1993, a truck bomb was exploded in the World Trade Center's underground garage. As he would do later, Rescorla oversaw the evacuation of the Morgan Stanley offices and went back to make sure everyone had escaped.

He recommended to his employers that the corporate offices be moved immediately. He thought the next terrorist attack would be with an airplane. But Morgan

Stanley's lease went through 2006, so his advice was ignored.

In his situation, some people might have resigned in frustration. But instead, Rescorla worked out an evacuation plan for the people at Morgan Stanley. At his insistence, *all* employees, including senior executives, practiced this emergency evacuation, walking down 44 flights of stairs, every three months.

And it's a good thing they did. When World Trade Center (WTC) Tower 1 was hit at 8:46 a.m. on Sept. 11, Rescorla ignored the official advice to stay put and began the orderly evacuation of Morgan Stanley's 2,700 employees on 20 floors of WTC Tower 2, and 1,000 employees in WTC 5.

When Tower 2 was hit by an airplane at 9:02 a.m., Rescorla had most of Morgan Stanley's employees, as well as many others, already evacuated to safety—*in less than 20 minutes*.

When told to evacuate himself, Rescorla replied, "As soon as I make sure everyone else is out," and went back in. He had been seen as high as the 72nd floor that morning. Right before Tower 2 collapsed, he was spotted on the 10th floor, heading upward.

Sept. 11 was not the first time that Rescorla's bravery and skills had been tested. A platoon leader in the 2nd Battalion, 7th Cavalry Regiment, 1st Cavalry Division (Airmobile), he served during the Vietnam War and took part in the bloody Battle of Ia Drang in 1965, which is described in the book and movie, *We Were Soldiers Once...And Young*. His men nicknamed him "Hard Core" for his bravery in battle and revered him for his good humor and compassion.

Lt. Gen. Hal Moore, who took part in the battle and co-authored the book, described Rescorla as "the best platoon leader I ever saw."

His decorations include the Silver Star, the Bronze Star with one oak leaf cluster, the Purple Heart and the Vietnamese Cross of Gallantry.

His actions on Sept. 11 came as no surprise to Vietnam veterans, who see his early recognition of the dangers at the World Trade Center and his insistence on being prepared as directly attributable to his military service. He was calm under fire, both when he served in Vietnam and when he led evacuation efforts on Sept. 11. He sang songs to keep people calm as they exited the towers, just as he had for his platoon in the Ia Drang Valley.

Of Morgan Stanley's 2,700 employees, all but six made it out that day. Four of those were Rescorla and his three deputies who were evacuating the buildings.

Rick Rescorla's bravery was exemplary on Sept. 11. But, in fact, it was just another chapter in a life punctuated with acts of courage and loyalty.

RICK RESCORLA left behind a wife, two children and three stepchildren.

There is an ongoing effort to award the Presidential Medal of Freedom to Rick Rescorla for heroism and gallantry beyond the call of duty on Sept. 11, 2001. As of this writing, there were more than 31,600 signatures on this petition. Visit: http://www.petitiononline.com/pmfrick/petition.html.

THE EDUCATION CENTER AT THE WALL

The Education Center at The Wall is an underground learning facility that will be built on the National Mall in Washington, D.C. near the Vietnam Veterans and Lincoln Memorials.

The Education Center will honor those who have put themselves in harm's way in all of America's wars and celebrate the values embodied by these brave and dedicated service members, using the Vietnam War as a lens through which to examine these characteristics.

The centerpiece of the exhibits will be a Wall of Faces, a multimedia display that will show the photos of the more than 58,000 whose names are on The Wall on their birthdays.

Other exhibits will show some of the more than 100,000 items left in tribute at the Memorial and provide a historical timeline for the Vietnam War and the creation of the Memorial.

Efforts are under way now to raise support for the project and collect photos and stories about the people whose names are on The Wall. To learn more, visit *www.buildthecenter.org* or call 1-866-990-WALL.

VIETNAM VETERANS MEMORIAL FUND

Established in 1979, the Vietnam Veterans Memorial Fund (VVMF) is the nonprofit organization authorized by Congress to build the Vietnam Veterans Memorial in Washington, D.C. Today, it works to preserve the legacy of The Wall, to promote healing and to educate about the impact of the Vietnam War through the following programs:

Ceremonies at The Wall are held each year on Memorial Day and Veterans Day to remember and honor those Americans who served in the armed forces. VVMF also holds ceremonies on Mother's Day, Father's Day and at Christmas.

In Memory honors those who died as a result of the Vietnam War, but whose deaths do not fit the parameters for inclusion on The Wall. A special ceremony is held on the third Monday of April each year.

The Wall That Heals brings the healing power of The Wall to cities and hometowns across America. The traveling half-scale replica of The Wall is accompanied by a traveling museum about the Vietnam War, The Wall and the era.

Echoes From The Wall is a curriculum kit sent free of charge to every middle and high school in America. It provides historical information about the Vietnam War, as well as an understanding of leadership, citizenship, patriotism and character.

Echoes From The Mall is a field trip guide that helps teachers interpret the Vietnam Veterans Memorial for their students in conjunction with class trips to Washington, D.C.

The Legacy of The Wall is a traveling storyboard that addresses several different aspects of the Vietnam War and the creation of The Wall.

The **Teach Vietnam Teachers Network** is comprised of educators throughout the United States who serve as liaisons between VVMF, their community and the school system. VVMF provides members with free educational materials and professional development opportunities.

Volunteers provide assistance to the Memorial's 4 million annual visitors—locating names, providing history lessons and helping with name rubbings. VVMF furnishes the necessary supplies for volunteers to continue their useful work.

Name Rubbings are provided free. Each week, volunteers bring paper and pencil to The Wall and begin the work to keep alive the memories of American heroes who made the ultimate sacrifice decades ago.

Memorial Preservation is maintained cooperatively between VVMF and the National Park Service. VVMF pays for catastrophic insurance for the Memorial as well as for annual name additions and status changes. Recently, it has funded improvements to various parts of the Memorial site and the upkeep of 13.5 acres of lawn at and around the Memorial. VVMF keeps granite panels in storage in case of damage to The Wall.

The Education Center at The Wall is VVMF's newest project. This underground learning center will be built on the National Mall in Washington, D.C., to show the pictures and tell the stories of the men and women who made the ultimate sacrifice in Vietnam.

The Vietnam Veterans Memorial Fund is a 501(c)(3) nonprofit organization, and its funding comes from grants and gifts from the general public. For more information, contact:

VIETNAM VETERANS MEMORIAL FUND
2600 Virginia Ave., NW, Suite 104
Washington, DC 20037
(202) 393-0090 *phone*
(202) 393-0029 *fax*
vvmf@vvmf.org
www.vvmf.org